Velociraptor

by Daniel Cohen

Consultant:
Brent Breithaupt
Director
Geological Museum
University of Wyoming

Bridgestone Books
an imprint of Capstone Press
Mankato, Minnesota

Bridgestone Books are published by Capstone Press
151 Good Counsel Drive, P.O. Box 669, Mankato, Minnesota 56002
http://www.capstone-press.com

Library of Congress Cataloging-in-Publication Data
Cohen, Daniel, 1936–
    Velociraptor/by Daniel Cohen.
    p. cm.—(The Bridgestone Science Library)
    Includes bibliographical references and index.
    Summary: Discusses the physical characteristics, habitat, food, defenses, relatives, and
extinction of the small but fierce meat-eating dinosaur that lived in prehistoric times.
    ISBN 0-7368-0621-0
    1. Velociraptor—Juvenile literature. [1. Velociraptor. 2. The Bridgestone Science Library.]
    I. Title. II. Series.
QE862.S3 V45 2001
567.912—dc21   00-021948

3 6626 10176 190 6

Editorial Credits
Erika Mikkelson, editor; Linda Clavel, cover designer and illustrator; Heidi Schoof
    and Kimberly Danger, photo researchers

Photo Credits
American Museum of Natural History, cover, 1, 14, 16, 20
Bowman Art Studio, 4
Frank DeNota, 6
Honolulu Community College, 10–11
The Natural History Museum/Orbis, 12
Visuals Unlimited/A. J. Copley, 8–9

Table of Contents

Velociraptor compared to a
5-foot-tall (1.5-meter-tall) human

Velociraptor

The name Velociraptor (vel-OSS-ih-RAP-tor) means speedy thief. This meat-eating dinosaur moved quickly. It may have stolen eggs from other dinosaurs. Velociraptor measured 6 feet (1.8 meters) from nose to tail and weighed about 33 pounds (15 kilograms).

The World of Velociraptor

Velociraptor lived about 80 million years ago. The dinosaur lived in the part of central Asia now called Mongolia. Many other small dinosaurs wandered this hot, dry land with Velociraptor.

This dinosaur is Deinonychus. Deinonychus and Velociraptor were dromaeosaurids.

Relatives of Velociraptor

The Velociraptor belonged to a group of dinosaurs called dromaeosaurids (DROHM-ee-oh-SORE-ids). These dinosaurs walked on two feet. Each foot had a curved claw. Dromaeosaurids had the largest brains of any dinosaur group.

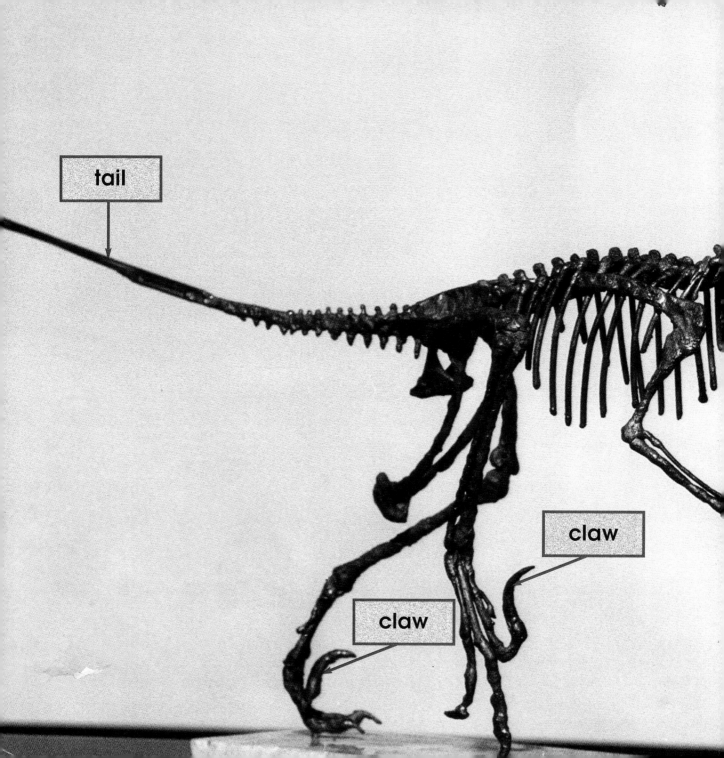

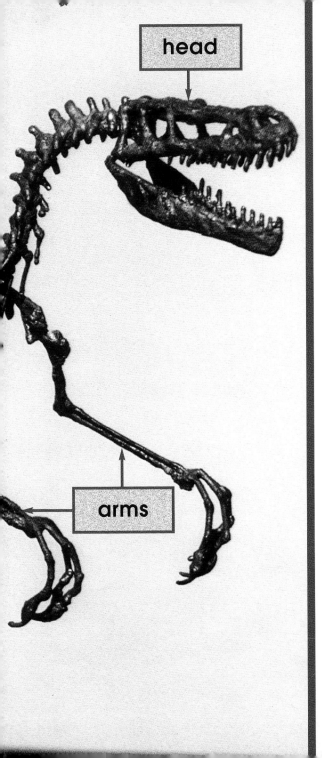

head

arms

Parts of Velociraptor

Velociraptor had a long head and a flat nose. Many sharp teeth filled its mouth. The dinosaur had two long arms and walked on two powerful legs. Velociraptor's claws looked like curved knives. Velociraptor had a stiff tail.

The End of Velociraptor

Velociraptor and its relatives became extinct about 70 million years ago. All other dinosaurs also died out about 65 million years ago. Scientists are not sure what caused the dinosaurs to die.

extinct
no longer living anywhere in the world

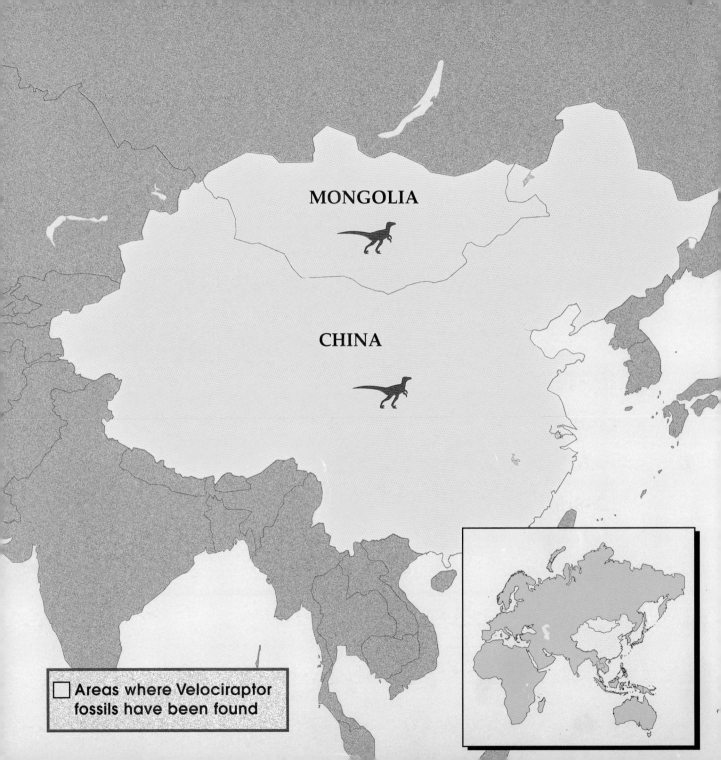

MONGOLIA

CHINA

☐ Areas where Velociraptor
fossils have been found

Discovering Velociraptor

In 1923, Peter Kaisen from the American Museum of Natural History discovered Velociraptor fossils in Mongolia. In 1924, paleontologist Henry Fairfield Osborn named the Velociraptor fossils. Paleontologists have found dromaeosaurid fossils in North America and parts of Asia.

paleontologist
a scientist who finds and studies fossils

Studying Velociraptor Today

Paleontologists continue to study
Velociraptor fossils. They want to learn
more about how fast the dinosaur ran.
They also are studying fossils to find
out how smart Velociraptor was.
Paleontologists hope to discover
how Velociraptor became extinct.

Hands On: Making a Fossil

Scientists have found impressions of fish and insects that lived millions of years ago. These prints appear on rocks or on the ground. Fossil impressions of plants tell scientists about the plants dinosaurs once ate. You can make your own fossil impressions.

What You Need

A ball of modeling clay
A small shell or leaf

What You Do

1. Flatten the ball of clay into a pancake shape.
2. Press or roll the shell or leaf firmly into the clay.
3. Carefully remove the shell or leaf.
4. Allow the clay to harden completely. The shape of the shell or leaf will remain in the hard clay.

Words to Know

dinosaur (DYE-na-sore)—an extinct land reptile; dinosaurs lived on Earth for more than 150 million years.

fossil (FOSS-uhl)—the remains or traces of something that once lived; bones and footprints can be fossils.

paleontologist (PAY-lee-on-TOL-ah-jist)—a scientist who finds and studies fossils

scientist (SYE-uhn-tist)—a person who studies the world around us

Read More

Landau, Elaine. *Velociraptor.* A True Book. New York: Children's Press, 1999.

Lessem, Don. *Raptors: The Nastiest Dinosaurs.* Boston: Little Brown, 1996.

Riehecky, Janet. *Velociraptor: The Swift Hunter.* Dinosaur Days. New York: Benchmark Books, 1998.

Internet Sites

Kinetosaurs: Dinosaur Database
http://www.childrensmuseum.org/kinetosaur/e.html
A Velociraptor Named Bambi
http://www.wmnh.com/wmbam000.htm
Zoom Dinosaurs
http://www.enchantedlearning.com/subjects/dinosaurs

Index